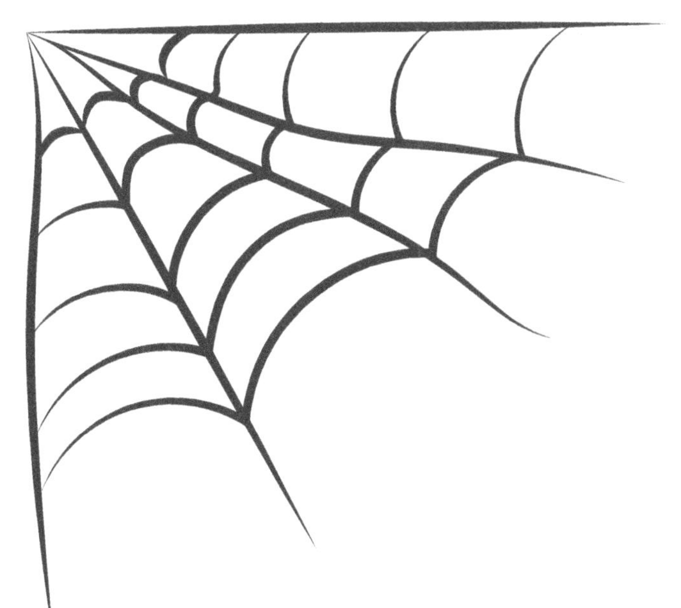

This grimoire belongs to

____

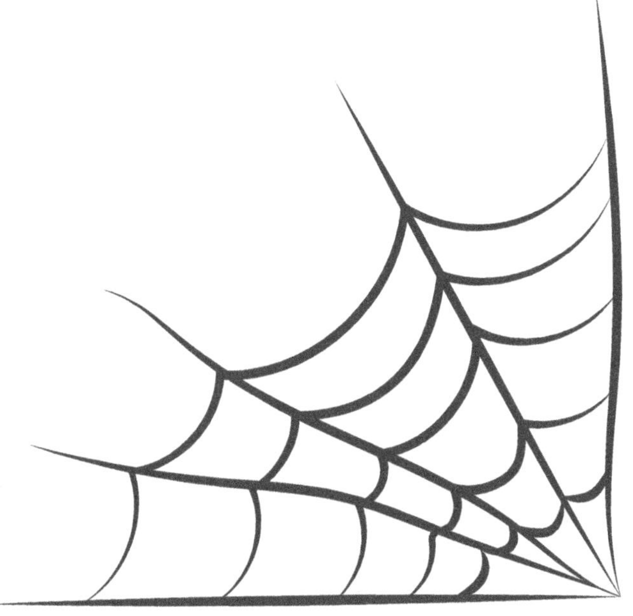

Hello there, and welcome to my witchy coloring book! I'm so glad you decided to pick it up. I Love witches and the way they can represent power, mystery, and creativity. I hope my coloring book can help you to tap into your own inner witch. I've tried to include a variety of different witchy illustrations in this book, so there's something for everyone.

I also wanted to take this opportunity to thank you for supporting my work. It means the world to me that you've chosen to buy my witchy coloring book. Your purchase will help me to continue creating art, and I'm so grateful for your support.

Thank you again for picking up my witchy coloring book! I hope you enjoy it.

Halloween

Thank you for coloring with me! I hope you enjoyed this witchy coloring book as much as I enjoyed creating it.

I know that coloring can be a great way to relax and de-stress, and I hope that this book has helped you to do just that. It's also a great way to let your creativity flow, and I hope that you've enjoyed exploring your inner witch through these pages.

I'm so grateful to you for supporting my work. Your purchase of this book will help me to continue creating art, and I'm so thankful for your support.

I hope you have many more relaxing and magical coloring sessions in the future.